Table Of Contents

Chapter 1: Introduction..1
Chapter 2: Setting Up Your Environment 1
Chapter 3: Building the Karaoke Player..1
Chapter 4: Singer Rotation and History 1
Chapter 5: Programming Independent Screens 1
Chapter 6: Advanced Features...1
Chapter 7: Testing and Deployment 1
Chapter 8: Conclusion 1
Table of Contents...1

Make your own Music

By: Chip Ziem (Karaoke Chip)

Table of Contents

1. Introduction

    - Overview of the Project
    - Why Use Python and PyCharm?
    - Features of the Karaoke Player

2. Setting Up Your Environment

    - Installing Python and PyCharm
    - Installing Required Libraries (e.g., Tkinter, SQLite, PyGame)

3. Building the Karaoke Player

    - Setting Up the Main Application Framework
    - Programming the Database Reader
    - Scanning Hard Drives for Karaoke Files

4. Singer Rotation and History

- Creating a Rotation System
- Saving and Loading Singer History

5. Programming Independent Screens

    - Screen 1: Singer Screen
    - Screen 2: Singer Rotation Screen
    - Screen 3: Audience Screen
    - Screen 4: Advertising Screen

6. Advanced Features

    - Implementing Key Changes for Songs
    - Adding Song Search Functionality

1. Testing and Deployment

    - Running the Karaoke Player
    - Exporting and Packaging the Application

2. Conclusion

    - Tips for Further Customization
    - Resources for Learning More

Chapter 1: Introduction

A professional karaoke player is an essential tool for DJs, event organizers, and karaoke enthusiasts. This chapter introduces the project, highlights the advantages of using Python and PyCharm, and outlines the features of the karaoke player you'll be building.

1.1 Overview of the Project

The karaoke player is designed to provide a seamless and interactive experience for both DJs and participants. The application will:

- Manage Songs: Automatically scan and store karaoke files from a hard drive into a database for easy access.
- Singer Rotation: Organize singers in a rotation list while tracking their favorite songs for quick retrieval.
- Independent Screens: Offer up to four separate screens for different purposes:

    1. Singer Screen: Displays the lyrics for the current singer.
    2. Rotation Screen: Shows the singer lineup and rotation order.
    3. Audience Screen: Displays lyrics or other visuals for the audience.
    4. Advertising Screen: Runs advertisements or announcements.

- Key Change: Adjust the song key to match singers' vocal ranges.

The karaoke player will be programmed using Python and PyCharm, offering a robust and scalable solution suitable for professional use.

1.2 Why Use Python and PyCharm?

Python is a popular programming language known for its simplicity, readability, and vast ecosystem of libraries. These characteristics make Python an excellent choice for building a karaoke player:

- Simplicity: Easy-to-read syntax reduces development time.
- Libraries: Access to powerful libraries for GUI design (Tkinter), database management (SQLite), and audio processing (PyGame).
- Community: A large developer community ensures ample resources and support.

PyCharm is an Integrated Development Environment (IDE) that enhances Python development by providing:

- Code Completion: Suggests and auto-completes code as you type.
- Debugging Tools: Helps identify and resolve issues quickly.
- Project Management: Organizes files and dependencies efficiently.

By combining Python and PyCharm, you can create a feature-rich karaoke player while improving your coding skills.

1.3 Features of the Karaoke Player

The karaoke player will include the following features:

1. Database Reader:

    - Automatically scans directories on a hard drive to identify karaoke files (e.g., .mp3, .kar).
    - Stores file metadata (title, artist, file path) in a SQLite database.

2. Singer Rotation and History:

    - Organizes singers in a rotation list to ensure everyone gets a turn.
    - Tracks singer preferences and displays favorite songs in their history.

3. Independent Screens:

    - Singer Screen: Displays lyrics and provides a timer for singers.
    - Rotation Screen: Keeps track of the next performers and their songs.
    - Audience Screen: Displays the lyrics and visuals for the crowd.
    - Advertising Screen: Shows promotional content or announcements.

4. Key Change Functionality:

   Adjusts the pitch of the song to match the singer's vocal range.

5. Ease of Use:

   - A clean, intuitive interface for DJs to manage the session efficiently.
   - Multiple configurations to suit different event types and setups.

1.4 Who Is This E-Book For?

This guide is intended for:

- Beginner Programmers: Those new to Python and looking for a practical project.
- Karaoke Enthusiasts: Individuals interested in creating a customized karaoke solution.
- DJs and Event Organizers: Professionals seeking a tailored karaoke player to enhance their events.

Even if you have minimal programming experience, this e-book provides clear instructions and detailed code examples to help you succeed.

1.5 What Will You Learn?

By the end of this e-book, you will have learned to:

1. Set up a Python development environment in PyCharm.
2. Use Python libraries to build a GUI, manage databases, and process audio.
3. Program independent screens for multi-purpose use.
4. Implement advanced features like singer rotation and key change.

This project will not only enhance your Python programming skills but also provide a functional tool you can use or customize for your specific needs.

1.6 How to Use This E-Book

To get the most out of this e-book:

1. Follow Along: Code each section in PyCharm as you read.
2. Experiment: Modify examples to understand how they work.
3. Complete Exercises: At the end of each chapter, try the suggested enhancements to solidify your learning.
4. Seek Support: Use the resources provided in the conclusion for additional guidance.

Chapter 2: Setting Up Your Environment

Before diving into coding, it's essential to set up a reliable development environment. This chapter walks you through installing Python, PyCharm, and the necessary libraries, ensuring you have everything ready to build your karaoke player.

2.1 Installing Python

Python is the foundation of this project. Follow these steps to install Python on your system:

1. Download Python:

    - Visit the official Python website: https://www.python.org/.
    - Download the latest stable version of Python for your operating system (Windows, macOS, or Linux).

2. Install Python:

    - Run the installer and ensure the checkbox "Add Python to PATH" is selected.
    - Choose the option for a standard installation or customize it if needed.

3. Verify Installation:

    - Open your terminal or command prompt and type:

    ```bash
    ```

    Copy code

    python --version

    - You should see the installed version of Python displayed.

2.2 Installing PyCharm

PyCharm is a powerful Integrated Development Environment (IDE) for Python development.

1. Download PyCharm:

    - Visit the JetBrains website: https://www.jetbrains.com/pycharm/.
    - Download the Community Edition (free) or the Professional Edition (paid with advanced features).

2. Install PyCharm:

    - Run the installer and follow the setup instructions.

- During installation, select the options to create a desktop shortcut and associate .py files with PyCharm.

3. Launch PyCharm:

   Open PyCharm and complete the initial setup by selecting your theme (light or dark) and installing any recommended plugins.

4. Create a New Project:

   - Click "New Project" on the welcome screen.
   - Choose a location for your project folder and configure the interpreter:
     - Select the Python interpreter installed earlier.
     - PyCharm will automatically create a virtual environment for your project.

2.3 Installing Required Libraries

For this project, you'll need several Python libraries to handle tasks like GUI design, database management, and audio playback. Install these libraries using the PyCharm terminal or your command prompt.

Libraries Needed

1. Tkinter: For building the graphical user interface.
2. SQLite3: For managing the song database.
3. PyGame: For audio playback and key adjustments.

Installation Commands

Open your terminal or PyCharm's built-in terminal and type the following commands:

```bash
```

Copy code

```
pip install pygame
```

2.4 Verifying Your Setup

Ensure everything is working correctly by running a simple test program:

1. Create a New Python File:

In your PyCharm project, right-click the project folder and select "New > Python File". Name it setup_test.py.

2. Write the Code:

```python
```

Copy code

import tkinter as tk import sqlite3 import pygame print("All libraries installed correctly!")

3. Run the Program:

   - Click the green Run button in PyCharm or press Shift+F10.
   - If there are no errors, your setup is complete.

2.5 Setting Up Version Control

Version control allows you to track changes in your project and collaborate with others. Using Git with GitHub is a common approach.

Install Git:

Download Git from https://git-scm.com/ and follow the installation instructions.

Initialize a Repository:

1. Open PyCharm and go to VCS > Enable Version Control Integration.
2. Select Git and click OK.
3. Commit your initial project files to track changes.

Push to GitHub:

1. Create a repository on GitHub (https://github.com/).
2. Follow the instructions to connect your local repository to GitHub.

2.6 Testing Your Environment

To ensure everything is working as expected, run this simple GUI program using Tkinter:

```python
```

Copy code

```python
import tkinter as tk # Create the main window root = tk.Tk() root.title("Environment Test") # Add a label label = tk.Label(root, text="Environment setup complete!", font=("Arial", 18)) label.pack(pady=20) # Start the GUI loop root.mainloop()
```

1. Save the file as test_gui.py.
2. Run it in PyCharm, and you should see a window displaying the text "Environment setup complete!".

Key Takeaways

- Python and PyCharm are the foundational tools for this project.
- Install the necessary libraries (Tkinter, SQLite3, PyGame) to ensure your application can handle GUIs, databases, and audio.
- Setting up version control with Git and GitHub helps you manage your project effectively.

Chapter 3: Building the Karaoke Player

This chapter focuses on the foundational components of the karaoke player, including the main application framework, a database reader, and a file scanner to manage your karaoke files. By the end of this chapter, you'll have a working base for your karaoke system.

3.1 Setting Up the Main Application Framework

The karaoke player's main application is built using the Tkinter library to create a graphical user interface (GUI).

Objective

- Create a basic GUI with navigation buttons to access different screens.
- Define the main application window and its layout.

Code Example: Main Framework

python

Copy code

```python
import tkinter as tk class KaraokeApp: def init(self, root): self.root = root self.root.title("Karaoke Player") self.root.geometry("800x600") # Main screen title tk.Label(self.root, text="Karaoke Player", font=("Arial", 24)).pack(pady=20) # Navigation buttons tk.Button(self.root, text="Singer Screen", command=self.open_singer_screen, width=20).pack(pady=10) tk.Button(self.root, text="Rotation Screen", command=self.open_rotation_screen, width=20).pack(pady=10) tk.Button(self.root, text="Audience Screen", command=self.open_audience_screen, width=20).pack(pady=10) tk.Button(self.root, text="Advertising Screen", command=self.open_advertising_screen, width=20).pack(pady=10) def open_singer_screen(self): print("Navigating to Singer Screen...") def open_rotation_screen(self): print("Navigating to Rotation Screen...") def open_audience_screen(self):
```

```
print("Navigating to Audience Screen...") def open_advertising_screen(self): print("Navigating to Advertising Screen...") # Run the application if name == "__main__": root = tk.Tk() app = KaraokeApp(root) root.mainloop()
```

Explanation

1. self.root: Represents the main application window.

2. Labels and Buttons:

    o A label displays the application title.
    o Buttons navigate to different screens using placeholder functions.

3. Screen Navigation:

    Functions like open_singer_screen will be expanded later to open independent screens.

3.2 Programming the Database Reader

The database reader scans your hard drive for karaoke files and stores metadata (e.g., title, artist, file path) in a SQLite database for easy access.

Objective

- Automatically detect karaoke files (.mp3, .kar).
- Store metadata in a database table.

Code Example: Database Reader

```
python
```

Copy code

```
import os import sqlite3 def setup_database(db_path): conn = sqlite3.connect(db_path) cursor = conn.cursor() # Create table for storing songs cursor.execute(''' CREATE TABLE IF NOT EXISTS songs ( id INTEGER PRIMARY KEY AUTOINCREMENT, title TEXT, artist TEXT, filepath TEXT ) ''') conn.commit() conn.close() def scan_files(directory, db_path): conn = sqlite3.connect(db_path) cursor = conn.cursor() # Scan directory for karaoke files for root, _, files in os.walk(directory): for file in files: if file.endswith((".mp3", ".kar")): filepath = os.path.join(root, file) title, artist = parsemetadata(file) cursor.execute("INSERT INTO songs (title, artist, filepath) VALUES (?, ?, ?)", (title, artist, filepath)) conn.commit() conn.close() def parse_metadata(filename): # Parse metadata from filename (e.g., "Artist - Title.mp3") parts = filename.split(" - ") if len(parts) == 2: artist, title = parts[0], parts[1].replace(".mp3", "").replace(".kar", "") return title.strip(), artist.strip() return filename.replace(".mp3", "").replace(".kar", ""), "Unknown Artist" # Example usage db_path = "karaoke.db" setup_database(db_path) scan_files("C:/Karaoke", db_path)
```

Explanation

1. setup_database(): Initializes the database and creates a table for storing songs.
2. scan_files(): Recursively scans directories for karaoke files and adds metadata to the database.
3. parse_metadata(): Extracts the title and artist from file names formatted as Artist - Title.

3.3 Scanning Hard Drives for Karaoke Files

The file scanner identifies all karaoke files on the hard drive and updates the database in real time.

Objective

- Extend the database reader to support real-time scanning.
- Provide a GUI for initiating scans.

Code Example: File Scanner GUI

python

Copy code

```
import tkinter as tk
from tkinter import filedialog
import threading

class FileScannerApp:
    def init(self, root):
        self.root = root
        self.db_path = "karaoke.db"
        tk.Label(self.root, text="Karaoke File Scanner", font=("Arial", 18)).pack(pady=20)
        tk.Button(self.root, text="Select Folder", command=self.select_folder).pack(pady=10)
        self.status_label = tk.Label(self.root, text="", font=("Arial", 12))
        self.status_label.pack(pady=10)
        # Set up database
        setup_database(self.db_path)

    def select_folder(self):
        folder = filedialog.askdirectory()
        if folder:
            self.status_label.config(text="Scanning files...")
            threading.Thread(target=self.scan_files, args=(folder,)).start()

    def scan_files(self, folder):
        scan_files(folder, self.db_path)
        self.status_label.config(text="Scan Complete!")

# Run the file scanner
if name == "__main__":
    root = tk.Tk()
    root.geometry("400x300")
    app = FileScannerApp(root)
    root.mainloop()
```

Explanation

1. Folder Selection: The filedialog.askdirectory() function allows users to select a folder for scanning.
2. Multithreading: The scanning process runs in a separate thread to keep the GUI responsive.
3. Status Updates: A label displays the scanning status.

Key Takeaways

- The main framework establishes the structure of the karaoke player.
- A database reader manages song metadata efficiently.
- The file scanner integrates a user-friendly interface for scanning karaoke files.

Chapter 4: Singer Rotation and History

Managing singer rotations efficiently is a critical part of running a successful karaoke session. This chapter explains how to program a rotation system that ensures fair turns, keeps track of past performances, and allows quick access to singers' favorite songs.

4.1 Creating a Rotation System

The rotation system organizes singers into a queue, ensuring everyone gets a turn. It allows:

- Adding new singers to the rotation.
- Automatically advancing to the next singer.
- Viewing the current rotation order.

Objective

- Use a queue (list) to manage the rotation.
- Provide functions to add, remove, and advance singers.

Code Example: Rotation System

```
python
```

Copy code

```python
class SingerRotation:
    def init(self):
        self.rotation = []
    def add_singer(self, name):
        self.rotation.append(name)
        print(f"Singer '{name}' added to the rotation.")
    def remove_singer(self, name):
        if name in self.rotation:
            self.rotation.remove(name)
            print(f"Singer '{name}' removed from the rotation.")
        else:
            print(f"Singer '{name}' not found in the rotation.")
    def next_singer(self):
        if self.rotation:
            current_singer = self.rotation.pop(0)
            self.rotation.append(current_singer)
            print(f"Next singer: {current_singer}")
        else:
            print("The rotation is empty.")
    def view_rotation(self):
        if self.rotation:
            print("Current rotation:")
            for i, singer in enumerate(self.rotation, start=1):
                print(f"{i}. {singer}")
        else:
            print("No singers in the rotation.")

# Example usage
rotation = SingerRotation()
rotation.add_singer("Alice")
rotation.add_singer("Bob")
rotation.view_rotation()
rotation.next_singer()
rotation.view_rotation()
```

Output:

```
vbnet
```

Copy code

Singer 'Alice' added to the rotation. Singer 'Bob' added to the rotation. Current rotation: 1. Alice 2. Bob Next singer: Alice Current rotation: 1. Bob 2. Alice

4.2 Saving and Loading Singer History

Singer history allows you to keep track of their favorite songs and previous performances. This data is stored in a SQLite database for persistence.

Objective

- Save singers' names, favorite songs, and past performance details.
- Retrieve this information when adding a returning singer to the rotation.

Code Example: Singer History

python

Copy code

```python
import sqlite3

class SingerHistory:
    def __init__(self, db_path):
        self.db_path = db_path
        self.setup_database()

    def setup_database(self):
        conn = sqlite3.connect(self.db_path)
        cursor = conn.cursor()
        # Create a table for singer history
        cursor.execute('''
            CREATE TABLE IF NOT EXISTS singer_history (
                id INTEGER PRIMARY KEY AUTOINCREMENT,
                name TEXT,
                song TEXT,
                date_added TEXT
            )
        ''')
        conn.commit()
        conn.close()

    def add_history(self, name, song):
        conn = sqlite3.connect(self.db_path)
        cursor = conn.cursor()
        cursor.execute("INSERT INTO singer_history (name, song, date_added) VALUES (?, ?, datetime('now'))", (name, song))
        conn.commit()
        conn.close()
        print(f"Added history for {name}: {song}")

    def view_history(self, name):
        conn = sqlite3.connect(self.db_path)
        cursor = conn.cursor()
        cursor.execute("SELECT song, date_added FROM singer_history WHERE name = ?", (name,))
        results = cursor.fetchall()
        conn.close()
        if results:
            print(f"History for {name}:")
            for song, date in results:
                print(f"- {song} (Added on {date})")
        else:
            print(f"No history found for {name}.")

# Example usage
history = SingerHistory("karaoke.db")
history.add_history("Alice", "Wonderwall")
history.add_history("Bob", "Bohemian Rhapsody")
history.view_history("Alice")
```

Output:

yaml

Copy code

```
Added history for Alice: Wonderwall
Added history for Bob: Bohemian Rhapsody
History for Alice:
- Wonderwall (Added on 2024-12-04)
```

4.3 Integration: Combining Rotation and History

The rotation system can be integrated with the singer history database. When adding a returning singer, their favorite songs can be displayed.

Code Example: Integration

python

Copy code

```python
class KaraokeManager:
    def init(self):
        self.rotation = SingerRotation()
        self.history = SingerHistory("karaoke.db")

    def add_singer_with_history(self, name):
        # Check history for favorite songs
        print(f"Adding {name} to rotation...")
        self.history.view_history(name)
        self.rotation.add_singer(name)

# Example usage
manager = KaraokeManager()
manager.add_singer_with_history("Alice")
manager.add_singer_with_history("Bob")
manager.rotation.view_rotation()
```

Output:

```vbnet
Adding Alice to rotation...
History for Alice:
- Wonderwall (Added on 2024-12-04)
Singer 'Alice' added to the rotation.
Adding Bob to rotation...
History for Bob:
- Bohemian Rhapsody (Added on 2024-12-04)
Singer 'Bob' added to the rotation.
Current rotation:
1. Alice
2. Bob
```

4.4 Adding a GUI for Singer Rotation

You can extend the rotation system to include a user-friendly interface with Tkinter.

Code Example: GUI for Singer Rotation

python

Copy code

```python
class SingerRotationGUI:
    def init(self, root):
        self.manager = KaraokeManager()
        self.root = root
        self.root.title("Singer Rotation")
        self.root.geometry("400x400")

        # Input for singer name
        self.name_entry = tk.Entry(self.root, width=30)
        self.name_entry.pack(pady=10)

        tk.Button(self.root, text="Add Singer", command=self.add_singer).pack(pady=5)
        tk.Button(self.root, text="Next Singer", command=self.next_singer).pack(pady=5)
        tk.Button(self.root, text="View Rotation", command=self.view_rotation).pack(pady=5)

        # Display area
        self.display = tk.Text(self.root, width=50, height=10)
        self.display.pack(pady=10)

    def add_singer(self):
        name = self.name_entry.get()
        if name:
            self.manager.add_singer_with_history(name)
            self.display.insert(tk.END, f"Singer '{name}' added.\n")

    def next_singer(self):
        self.manager.rotation.next_singer()
        self.display.insert(tk.END, "Advanced to the next singer.\n")

    def view_rotation(self):
        self.display.delete(1.0, tk.END)
        rotation = self.manager.rotation.rotation
        self.display.insert(tk.END, "Current Rotation:\n")
        for i, singer in enumerate(rotation, start=1):
            self.display.insert(tk.END, f"{i}. {singer}\n")

# Run the application
if name == "__main__":
    root = tk.Tk()
    app = SingerRotationGUI(root)
    root.mainloop()
```

Key Takeaways

- The rotation system ensures fair turns and smooth management of singers.
- Singer history adds personalization by remembering favorite songs and past performances.

- A GUI enhances usability for DJs and event organizers.

Chapter 5: Programming Independent Screens

In this chapter, we will create up to four independent screens for different purposes:

1. Singer Screen: Displays lyrics for the current singer.
2. Rotation Screen: Shows the lineup and rotation order.
3. Audience Screen: Projects lyrics or visuals for the audience.
4. Advertising Screen: Displays advertisements or announcements.

Each screen will run independently, allowing for seamless transitions and efficient control.

5.1 Creating Independent Windows

To implement multiple screens, we'll use Tkinter's Toplevel widget. This allows you to create new windows separate from the main application.

Code Example: Basic Independent Windows

```python
```

Copy code

```python
import tkinter as tk

class IndependentScreensApp:
    def init(self, root):
        self.root = root
        self.root.title("Karaoke Main Controller")
        self.root.geometry("400x300")
        # Main window buttons
        tk.Button(self.root, text="Open Singer Screen", command=self.open_singer_screen).pack(pady=10)
        tk.Button(self.root, text="Open Rotation Screen", command=self.open_rotation_screen).pack(pady=10)
        tk.Button(self.root, text="Open Audience Screen", command=self.open_audience_screen).pack(pady=10)
        tk.Button(self.root, text="Open Advertising Screen", command=self.open_advertising_screen).pack(pady=10)

    def open_singer_screen(self):
        singer_window = tk.Toplevel(self.root)
        singer_window.title("Singer Screen")
        singer_window.geometry("800x600")
        tk.Label(singer_window, text="Singer Lyrics Here", font=("Arial", 24)).pack(pady=20)

    def open_rotation_screen(self):
        rotation_window = tk.Toplevel(self.root)
        rotation_window.title("Rotation Screen")
        rotation_window.geometry("800x600")
        tk.Label(rotation_window, text="Singer Rotation Order", font=("Arial", 24)).pack(pady=20)

    def open_audience_screen(self):
        audience_window = tk.Toplevel(self.root)
        audience_window.title("Audience Screen")
        audience_window.geometry("800x600")
        tk.Label(audience_window, text="Audience View", font=("Arial", 24)).pack(pady=20)

    def open_advertising_screen(self):
        advertising_window = tk.Toplevel(self.root)
        advertising_window.title("Advertising Screen")
        advertising_window.geometry("800x600")
        tk.Label(advertising_window, text="Advertisements Here", font=("Arial", 24)).pack(pady=20)

# Run the application
if name == "__main__":
    root = tk.Tk()
    app = IndependentScreensApp(root)
    root.mainloop()
```

Explanation

1. Toplevel Widget: Creates a new window independent of the main window.

2. Separate Functionality: Each screen has its own layout and can be customized for its purpose.

5.2 Singer Screen: Displaying Lyrics

The Singer Screen displays lyrics for the current singer. This includes:

- Showing lyrics in real-time.
- Allowing scrolling or line-by-line progression.

Code Example: Singer Screen with Lyrics

python

Copy code

```python
class SingerScreen:
    def init(self, parent):
        self.window = tk.Toplevel(parent)
        self.window.title("Singer Screen")
        self.window.geometry("800x600")
        # Display lyrics
        self.lyrics_text = tk.Text(self.window, font=("Arial", 16), wrap=tk.WORD)
        self.lyrics_text.pack(expand=True, fill=tk.BOTH)
        # Control buttons
        tk.Button(self.window, text="Load Lyrics", command=self.load_lyrics).pack(pady=5)
        tk.Button(self.window, text="Clear Lyrics", command=self.clear_lyrics).pack(pady=5)

    def load_lyrics(self):
        lyrics = """Here's an example of karaoke lyrics:
        Twinkle, twinkle, little star,
        How I wonder what you are.
        Up above the world so high,
        Like a diamond in the sky."""
        self.lyrics_text.insert(tk.END, lyrics)

    def clear_lyrics(self):
        self.lyrics_text.delete(1.0, tk.END)
```

Features

- Text Widget: Displays lyrics with word wrapping.
- Control Buttons: Load and clear lyrics dynamically.

5.3 Rotation Screen: Displaying Lineup

The Rotation Screen shows the singer lineup and their selected songs.

Code Example: Rotation Screen

python

Copy code

```python
class RotationScreen:
    def init(self, parent, rotation_list):
        self.window = tk.Toplevel(parent)
        self.window.title("Rotation Screen")
        self.window.geometry("800x600")
        # Display rotation order
        tk.Label(self.window, text="Singer Rotation", font=("Arial", 24)).pack(pady=10)
        self.listbox = tk.Listbox(self.window, font=("Arial", 16), width=40, height=20)
        self.listbox.pack(pady=10)
        # Populate rotation
        for singer in rotation_list:
            self.listbox.insert(tk.END, singer)

    def update_rotation(self, rotation_list):
        self.listbox.delete(0, tk.END)
        for singer in rotation_list:
            self.listbox.insert(tk.END, singer)
```

Features

- Listbox Widget: Displays the current rotation order.
- Dynamic Updates: Easily refresh the list when the rotation changes.

5.4 Audience Screen: Visuals for the Crowd

The Audience Screen provides lyrics or visual effects for the audience.

Code Example: Audience Screen

python

Copy code

```python
class AudienceScreen:
    def init(self, parent):
        self.window = tk.Toplevel(parent)
        self.window.title("Audience Screen")
        self.window.geometry("800x600")
        # Display content
        self.label = tk.Label(self.window, text="Audience View", font=("Arial", 32), fg="blue")
        self.label.pack(expand=True)
    def update_content(self, text):
        self.label.config(text=text)
```

Features

- Large, customizable text for easy viewing.
- Option to dynamically update content for audience engagement.

5.5 Advertising Screen: Displaying Ads

The Advertising Screen cycles through advertisements or announcements.

Code Example: Advertising Screen

python

Copy code

```python
import time
class AdvertisingScreen:
    def init(self, parent):
        self.window = tk.Toplevel(parent)
        self.window.title("Advertising Screen")
        self.window.geometry("800x600")
        # Ad content
        self.ads = ["Ad 1: Special Discount on Drinks!", "Ad 2: Karaoke Night Every Friday!", "Ad 3: Book Your Event with Us!"]
        self.label = tk.Label(self.window, text="", font=("Arial", 24), fg="green")
        self.label.pack(expand=True)
        # Cycle ads
        self.current_ad = 0
        self.cycle_ads()
    def cycle_ads(self):
        self.label.config(text=self.ads[self.current_ad])
        self.current_ad = (self.current_ad + 1) % len(self.ads)
        self.window.after(5000, self.cycle_ads)  # Update ad every 5 seconds
```

Features

- Cycles through advertisements automatically.
- Configurable timing for ad transitions.

Key Takeaways

- Each screen is designed to operate independently, offering flexibility for DJs.
- Screens are tailored for specific functions: singers, audience, rotation management, and advertising.
- Using Toplevel, you can create multiple windows that interact seamlessly.

Chapter 6: Advanced Features

In this chapter, we'll implement advanced functionalities to enhance your karaoke player. These include:

1. Key Change Functionality: Adjust the song pitch to match singers' vocal ranges.
2. Adding a Song Search Feature: Allow DJs to quickly find songs from the database.
3. Enhancing User Experience: Adding features like timers and background themes.

6.1 Implementing Key Change Functionality

Key change functionality adjusts the pitch of a song in real-time to match the singer's vocal range. This feature uses the PyGame library for audio playback and manipulation.

Objective

- Allow the DJ to increase or decrease the song pitch (key).
- Ensure the audio playback is seamless during key changes.

Code Example: Key Change with PyGame

```
python
```

Copy code

```
import pygame class KeyChangePlayer: def init(self, file_path): self.file_path = file_path self.key = 0 # Default pitch pygame.mixer.init() def load_song(self): pygame.mixer.music.load(self.file_path) print(f"Loaded song: {self.file_path}") def play_song(self): pygame.mixer.music.play() print("Playing song...") def stop_song(self): pygame.mixer.music.stop() print("Song stopped.") def change_key(self, semitones): self.key += semitones print(f"Key changed by {self.key} semitones.") # Simulated key change: PyGame does not directly support key shifts; use external libraries (e.g., PySound or PyDub) for real pitch manipulation. # Example Usage player = KeyChangePlayer("path/to/song.mp3") player.load_song() player.play_song() player.change_key(2) # Increase pitch by 2 semitones player.stop_song()
```

Enhancement Ideas

- Integrate a slider in the GUI to allow real-time key adjustments.
- Use advanced libraries like PyDub for accurate pitch changes.

6.2 Adding a Song Search Feature

The song search feature allows the DJ to quickly find songs by title or artist.

Objective

- Enable efficient querying of the song database.
- Provide a GUI for searching and displaying results.

Code Example: Song Search

python

Copy code

```python
import sqlite3
class SongSearch:
    def init(self, db_path):
        self.db_path = db_path
    def search_songs(self, query):
        conn = sqlite3.connect(self.db_path)
        cursor = conn.cursor()
        cursor.execute("SELECT title, artist FROM songs WHERE title LIKE ? OR artist LIKE ?", (f"%{query}%", f"%{query}%"))
        results = cursor.fetchall()
        conn.close()
        return results
# Example Usage
search = SongSearch("karaoke.db")
results = search.search_songs("love")
print("Search Results:")
for title, artist in results:
    print(f"Title: {title}, Artist: {artist}")
```

GUI Integration

python

Copy code

```python
class SongSearchGUI:
    def init(self, root, db_path):
        self.search = SongSearch(db_path)
        self.root = root
        self.root.title("Song Search")
        self.root.geometry("500x400")
        tk.Label(self.root, text="Search Songs", font=("Arial", 18)).pack(pady=10)
        self.search_entry = tk.Entry(self.root, width=30)
        self.search_entry.pack(pady=5)
        tk.Button(self.root, text="Search", command=self.perform_search).pack(pady=5)
        self.results_list = tk.Listbox(self.root, width=50, height=15)
        self.results_list.pack(pady=10)
    def perform_search(self):
        query = self.search_entry.get()
        results = self.search.search_songs(query)
        self.results_list.delete(0, tk.END)
        for title, artist in results:
            self.results_list.insert(tk.END, f"{title} - {artist}")
# Run the GUI
if name == "__main__":
    root = tk.Tk()
    app = SongSearchGUI(root, "karaoke.db")
    root.mainloop()
```

6.3 Adding Timers and Visual Effects

Timers help manage performance durations, while visual effects improve user experience.

Objective

- Display a timer for each singer's performance.
- Use animations or transitions to enhance the interface.

Code Example: Timer for Singer Screen

python

Copy code

```
class Timer:
    def init(self, root, duration):
        self.root = root
        self.duration = duration
        self.label = tk.Label(self.root, text="", font=("Arial", 24))
        self.label.pack(pady=20)
        self.start_timer()

    def start_timer(self):
        if self.duration > 0:
            minutes, seconds = divmod(self.duration, 60)
            self.label.config(text=f"{minutes:02}:{seconds:02}")
            self.duration -= 1
            self.root.after(1000, self.start_timer)
        else:
            self.label.config(text="Time's up!")

# Run Timer
if name == "__main__":
    root = tk.Tk()
    root.geometry("300x200")
    timer = Timer(root, 120)  # 2-minute timer
    root.mainloop()
```

Visual Effects

For advanced visuals, integrate libraries like Tkinter Canvas or PyGame:

python

Copy code

```
# Example: Flashing Text on Canvas
canvas = tk.Canvas(root, width=500, height=300)
canvas.pack()
text = canvas.create_text(250, 150, text="Let's Sing!", font=("Arial", 32), fill="blue")

def flash_text():
    current_color = canvas.itemcget(text, "fill")
    new_color = "red" if current_color == "blue" else "blue"
    canvas.itemconfig(text, fill=new_color)
    root.after(500, flash_text)

flash_text()
```

6.4 Customizing Themes and Layouts

Enhance the karaoke player's appearance with themes and layouts.

Objective

- Customize colors, fonts, and backgrounds for different screens.
- Provide options for users to switch themes.

Code Example: Theme Selector

python

Copy code

```
class ThemeManager: def init(self, root): self.root = root self.current_theme = "Light" tk.Button(self.root, text="Switch Theme", command=self.switch_theme).pack(pady=10) def switch_theme(self): if self.current_theme == "Light": self.root.config(bg="black") self.current_theme = "Dark" else: self.root.config(bg="white") self.current_theme = "Light" # Run Theme Selector if name == "__main__": root = tk.Tk() root.geometry("400x300") app = ThemeManager(root) root.mainloop()
```

Key Takeaways

- Key change functionality adds professional-grade customization for singers.
- A search feature enhances usability by allowing quick access to songs.
- Timers and visual effects improve organization and audience engagement.
- Customizable themes provide a polished, user-friendly interface.

Chapter 7: Testing and Deployment

After completing the core development of the karaoke player, it's time to test its functionality and prepare it for deployment. This chapter covers:

1. Testing the Karaoke Player: Identifying and fixing bugs.
2. Packaging the Application: Creating an executable file for easy distribution.
3. Deploying the Karaoke Player: Steps to deploy on different systems.

7.1 Testing the Karaoke Player

Testing ensures your application works as intended and meets user requirements.

1. Unit Testing

Unit tests check individual components of the application, such as the database reader or singer rotation system.

Example: Unit Test for the Database Reader

python

Copy code

```
import unittest import os import sqlite3 from karaoke_player.database_reader import setup_database, scan_files class TestDatabaseReader(unittest.TestCase): def setUp(self): # Create a test database self.db_path = "test_karaoke.db" setup_database(self.db_path) def tearDown(self): # Clean up the test database if os.path.exists(self.db_path): os.remove(self.db_path) def test_scan_files(self): # Scan a test folder os.makedirs("test_songs", exist_ok=True) with open("test_songs/Sample - Song.mp3", "w") as f: f.write("Dummy file content") scan_files("test_songs", self.db_path) # Check if the file was added to the database conn = sqlite3.connect(self.db_path) cursor = conn.cursor() cursor.execute("SELECT COUNT(*) FROM songs") count = cursor.fetchone()[0] conn.close() self.assertEqual(count, 1) if name == "__main__": unittest.main()
```

2. Integration Testing

Integration tests ensure that different components (e.g., screens, database, and audio playback) work together.

Example: Integration Test for Screen Navigation

python

Copy code

class TestScreenNavigation(unittest.TestCase): def test_navigation(self): app = KaraokeApp(tk.Tk()) app.open_singer_screen() app.open_rotation_screen() self.assertIsNotNone(app.root)

3. Manual Testing

Manual testing involves using the karaoke player to simulate real-world scenarios:

- Load and play songs.
- Add singers to the rotation.
- Test key changes during playback.
- Use all screens to ensure they function independently.

7.2 Packaging the Application

To make your karaoke player easy to use, package it into a standalone executable file. This avoids requiring users to install Python or dependencies.

Using PyInstaller

PyInstaller is a popular tool for converting Python scripts into standalone executables.

1. Install PyInstaller:

   bash

   Copy code

   pip install pyinstaller

2. Package the Karaoke Player:

   - Navigate to your project directory in the terminal and run:

```bash
Copy code

pyinstaller --onefile --noconsole main.py
```

- o The --onefile flag creates a single executable file.
- o The --noconsole flag suppresses the terminal for GUI applications.

3. Find the Executable:

After the process completes, the executable file will be located in the dist folder.

4. Test the Executable:

Run the executable on different systems to ensure it works without errors.

7.3 Deploying the Karaoke Player

Deployment involves distributing your application to end-users.

1. Deployment on Windows

- Package the executable with all required assets (e.g., database, media files) in a folder.
- Use Inno Setup to create an installer:
    1. Download and install Inno Setup from https://jrsoftware.org/.
    2. Write a script to package your application.
    3. Generate an installer.

2. Deployment on macOS

- Use PyInstaller to generate a macOS .app package:

```bash
Copy code

pyinstaller --onefile --windowed main.py
```

- Test the .app file on macOS to ensure compatibility.

3. Deployment on Linux

- Use PyInstaller to create a Linux executable:

bash

Copy code

pyinstaller --onefile main.py

- Create a .deb package using tools like dpkg-deb.

4. Distributing Updates

Use version control tools like GitHub or GitLab to distribute updates. You can:

- Tag releases for specific versions.
- Provide downloadable executables.

7.4 Error Logging and Reporting

Add error logging to your application to capture issues during runtime. This will help in debugging and improve the user experience.

Code Example: Error Logging

python

Copy code

```
import logging # Configure logging logging.basicConfig( filename="karaoke_player.log", level=logging.ERROR, format="%(asctime)s - %(levelname)s - %(message)s" ) try: # Example function that may raise an error def faulty_function(): raise ValueError("An error occurred.") faulty_function() except Exception as e: logging.error("An unexpected error occurred.", exc_info=True)
```

7.5 User Documentation

Provide user documentation to help end-users understand how to use the karaoke player. Include:

1. Getting Started: Instructions for installation and setup.
2. Using the Application:
    - How to add singers.
    - Navigating screens.
    - Adjusting song keys.

3. Troubleshooting:

    o Common errors and their solutions.
    o How to report issues.

Key Takeaways

- Comprehensive testing ensures the reliability of your application.
- Packaging with PyInstaller creates user-friendly executables.
- Deployment strategies vary based on the operating system.
- Error logging and user documentation enhance the overall experience for end-users.

Chapter 8: Conclusion

Congratulations on reaching the conclusion of this e-book! By now, you have built a fully functional karaoke player equipped with advanced features and independent screens, tailored for professional DJ use. This chapter summarizes what you've accomplished, provides tips for further learning, and suggests enhancements you can explore to take your project to the next level.

8.1 What You Have Accomplished

Let's reflect on the journey you've completed:

1. Environment Setup:

    Installed Python and PyCharm, and configured the development environment with the necessary libraries.

2. Main Application Framework:

    Built a robust GUI using Tkinter to manage singers, display lyrics, and interact with the karaoke system.

3. Database Management:

    Created a SQLite database to manage song metadata and singer history.

4. Singer Rotation and History:

    Implemented a fair rotation system and history tracking to enhance user experience.

5. Independent Screens:

    Developed four independent screens for singers, audience, rotation management, and advertising.

6. Advanced Features:

    Added key change functionality, a song search tool, and dynamic timers.

1. Testing and Deployment:

    Ensured reliability through unit and integration testing and prepared the application for distribution.

These milestones demonstrate your growth as a Python programmer and your ability to develop real-world applications.

8.2 Tips for Enhancing Your Karaoke Player

While the karaoke player you've built is functional and versatile, there are many opportunities to enhance its features:

1. Real-Time Lyrics Syncing

- Implement a lyrics syncing feature that highlights each line in time with the music.
- Use libraries like PyDub or time to achieve precise timing.

2. Multi-User Networking

- Enable multiple users to connect to the karaoke player over a local network or the internet.
- Use the socket library or frameworks like Flask to build a web-based interface for adding singers or browsing songs remotely.

3. Enhanced Visual Effects

- Add animations or background themes for the audience screen.
- Use the Canvas widget in Tkinter or external libraries like Pyglet to create more dynamic visuals.

4. Integration with Streaming Services

- Allow DJs to import songs directly from platforms like YouTube or Spotify.
- Use APIs (e.g., YouTube Data API) to fetch karaoke tracks.

5. Voice Processing

- Integrate real-time voice processing to adjust microphone levels or add effects like echo or reverb.
- Explore libraries like SoundDevice or PyAudio for audio manipulation.

6. Mobile App Integration

- Develop a companion mobile app for audience members to view the rotation list, suggest songs, or vote on performances.
- Use tools like Flask for the backend and React Native or Flutter for mobile development.

8.3 Resources for Further Learning

Your journey doesn't stop here. Continue building your programming skills with the following resources:

Python Programming

1. "Automate the Boring Stuff with Python" by Al Sweigart: A beginner-friendly guide to practical Python programming.
2. Python Documentation: https://docs.python.org - The official Python documentation.

GUI Development

1. Tkinter Documentation: https://tkdocs.com/
2. Kivy Framework: https://kivy.org/ - For creating advanced, multi-touch applications.

Database Management

1. SQLite Documentation: https://sqlite.org/docs.html
2. SQLAlchemy: A more advanced database toolkit for Python (https://sqlalchemy.org/).

Audio and Media Processing

1. PyDub: https://github.com/jiaaro/pydub
2. PyGame: https://www.pygame.org/ - For building interactive audio-visual applications.

Networking and APIs

1. Flask Framework: https://flask.palletsprojects.com/
2. Requests Library: https://docs.python-requests.org/ - For interacting with web APIs.

8.4 Final Words

You've built more than just a karaoke player—you've created a professional-grade tool that showcases your programming skills and problem-solving abilities. As you continue to develop your expertise, remember:

- Experiment Fearlessly: Modify the application, try new libraries, and explore uncharted territories in programming.
- Learn from Challenges: Every bug or error is an opportunity to deepen your understanding.
- Share Your Work: Publish your karaoke player on platforms like GitHub or share it with friends to gather feedback and improve.

Python's versatility ensures endless possibilities for projects like this one. Keep coding, keep learning, and who knows—you might create the next big thing in karaoke software!

www.ingramcontent.com/pod-product-compliance
Lightning Source LLC
Chambersburg PA
CBHW082258220526
45469CB00009B/3061